How Much Can I See: Faith Over Fear

Michele Farrell

Presentation by *BookLeaf Publishing*

Web: www.bookleafpub.com

E-mail: info@bookleafpub.com

ISBN: 9789357441674

First edition 2023

Danny, thank you for being my strength, my shield, and my shoulder. I love you.

PREFACE

Welcome reader and thank you for joining me as I share my life, my love, and my search for happiness through the "art of poetry". If God, love, and family offend you...TURN BACK NOW!

Live

Open your eyes!
Are you spiritually paralyzed?
Christ died
So YOU can thrive
It's time to strive for better
Together
Or apart
Let's start
Now, not later
You're no waiter.
Fuck the haters
You're blessed…
God's ticket to success
Paid in advance
Covering sin and circumstances
So, take chances
Not glances

Peter 1 Chapter 1
All praise to God, the Father of our Lord Jesus
Christ. It is by his great mercy that we have been
born again, because God raised Jesus Christ
from the dead. Now we live with great
expectation.

Critics

Do you see me?
My inner beauty not just my booty
My pure heart
Did you know I'm also smart
Where did you want to start?
In my bed,
In my head,
Or am I jumping ahead?
Critics, y'all are everywhere
Judging my clothes, home, and hair
It's truly hard not to care
I feel the judgement in your stare
I'm learning it's okay
To ignore what you say.
When push comes to shove
I know what I'm made of
I might bend but not break.
God knows what I can take.
I'm no angel
This is fine
I was created with God's design.
It's okay that you don't see me
Because God's love shaped me.
Five years from now…
I'm who you'll want to be.

Nobody Love

You are my home
Thanks to you...
I'm never alone
When you called my phone
I heard your tone...
You needed to be shown
How to heal from the pain
Caused by the ex that drove you insane.
As for me...
I needed to see...
Someone love me wholeheartedly.
You help me conquer my fears
You dry my tears
You show me you care
I know you'll always be there
Your love is fair
You're aware
I'm not going anywhere

People told me it's not smart
To give you my heart
So glad I didn't listen
Because your love isn't worth missing
Out on
Nor the talks from dark to dawn

I feel i need to say
Your love makes me better
Day by day
And I plan to love you
In each and every way.

My Dream or Your Reality

The storm rages in the night
I'm jolted awake
My mind in fright
My husband lays next to me
Sleeping peacefully
My body is frozen
Due to fear
My left eye loses...
Just one tear
The thunder booms,
The ground shakes,
And Indiana has an earthquake
I need to scream
I need to shout
I need to let the terror out
I hear a "bang"
I hear a "crash"
The end will be here...
In a flash
It's not a "drill"
It's not a "dream"
My heart is racing
I want to scream
Lightening lights the room
The executioner's blade strikes soon

It will not slow
It will not dally
The grim reaper always…
Gets his tally
"I'm not ready"
"I need more time"
Are the thoughts
On my mind
Just ONE look
Just ONE glance
Tells me there's no "second chance"
My current predicament
Should come with comments
Instead of just Him,
His knife,
And a scared wife.
Suddenly, i see a spark
The room goes dark,
I'm torn apart,
And I begin…
My afterlife free of sin
Another boom…
And I awaken
Sweaty, panting, and shaken.
My husband wakes with a "scream"
To say…
"My love, you died in my dream."

I'm NOT Nothing

I'm a bitch
I'm a tease
I'm a goddess on my knees
I will rant
I will rage
I will NOT be caged
I'm a renegade
I'm insane
Results from life's pain
I know death
Good health
And a sense of self
Worth…
On earth
I desire
To light a fire
And watch it burn
While the world learns
Not to underestimate me
I want to cry
Each time I try
To be seen,
To be found
To hear just ONE sound
Of acceptance

Of truth
To annihilate the damage
Took on in my youth
So i dance
And i sing
As a reminder…
I'm NOT nothing

Genesis

Tell me,
When does life begin?
Is it when you crawl?
Is it when you walk?
Is it when you learn to talk?
When does life begin?
Does it begin after your first win?
Or after your first loss?
Does it begin after you cross...that Stage?
When does life begin?
Take a page...from my book...
It only takes a second to look...
To see...
life's true beauty.
When does life begin?
There's no answer when...
You know...
Where your loved ones go.
After you've cried
Because they've died
When does life begin?
Many people are divided...
But life begins when
You're reunited
With something you lost…

With that love you found…
When does life begin?
There's no real answer that you'll find.
But if you'd like to try…
First,
Search your mind.

Queen P

Have you met a Queen?
You know who I mean.
She's fun
She's flirty
She's a bit nerdy
She's fierce
She's vicious
She cooks, cleans, and does dishes
She's a pillar of strength
She prefers a man with "length"
She's honest
She's fare
She'll handle you with care
She's a Diva
She's kind
She's always on my mind
She's faithful
She's a great friend
Take it from me
In her heart is...
"The place to be"

Fight or Flight

I sit and contemplate
How to uncomplicate
The damaging thoughts
I was taught
To ignore
For...you...
A man who
Broke my heart in two
Pieces of me
You cannot see
Because I bury pain...
Effortlessly
You'll NEVER know what it's like
Because you NEVER had to fight
You lie,
You cheat,
And you steal
It's unreal...
The "praise" you received
For raising me
You know...
The child you couldn't see
Did you know
Your sons bullied me?
Keeping my "cool"

At home and in school
Was so illogical
And almost impossible
Thank God for my only friend
Who loved me even when
I couldn't love myself
Because someone else asked me
"How much can you see?"
That question almost ruined me.
It seems wrong
To sing a "happy song"
Now that you're gone.
I don't care though
I just want you know...
I used that pain
To "set fire to the rain"
Now I am the "flame"
I burn bright
And I NO longer feel the need for
Fight or flight

One Day

One day,
I had a reason
To stop breathin'
I could barely maintain
I was going insane...
I lost you before you were mine
We didn't get enough time...
Together.
My love wasn't enough
To whether the storm
And you were never…
Born.
Years later and I still morn
The blessing I lost.
One day,
The pain will fade away.
But is that okay?
Or should it hurt forever?
Damn…
I gotta get it together.
One day,
I awoke
And didn't choke
On the thought of you.
So, it must be true…

God's love heals heartache too.
One day,
What you meant to me
Will eventually…
Be a memory.

May 6th

I walk down the aisle
Wearing a thousand watt smile
Wearing that white dress
And a stomach full of butterflies
Surrounded by loved ones
With tears in their eyes
My brother's arm steadies me
While I march toward my destiny,
My king,
My all,
And my everything.
You are my confidant,
My friend,
The one I depend…
On
When I'm not strong.
In sickness and in health
You know me better…
Than I know myself.
You are truly a dream…
Come true
And I'd hate living life…
Without you.
You're handsome
And you sing.

I know I don't deserve…
This ring.
Because you're funny
And you're kind.
You must be out your mind.
To have chosen me.
A black girl from…
An Arkansas city.
But everyday you show…
There's nowhere you'd go…
Without me.
Because on May 6th…
We became family.

True Friends

True friends are hard to find
Because some people are mean
And some are kind
True friends are hard to define
Because what you require from your friends
May not be what I need from mine
True friends come with bonds unbroken
True friends keep secrets unspoken
True friends transcend time and space
True friends fortify you with love and grace
True friends are a safe place
A true friend is a treasure
One to cherish forever

Wonder Twin

Life is full of ups and downs
Can't believe you stuck around
You've seen me a my best and worst
You proved I wasn't cursed
We bonded over health trauma
And family drama
You don't judge or criticize…
The fact I can't use my eyes
You hold me together…
In good and bad weather
You bring joy and laughter to my life
You stood at my side when I became a wife
You lift me up when I'm feeling low
You're always there to watch me grow
You show me what it means to care
You my friend…
Are truly rare
You my friend…you're pure and true
You my friend…bless ALL who know you

Thank you, Ex

I gave you my heart
But you gave nothing back
Loving you...
Caused my heart attack.
You wanted me there…
You convinced me you cared
Loving you…made me drown
But I couldn't make a sound
When we fought…you'd ignore me
You even talked to someone else…
While I was home by myself
Instead of affection and love…
All you brought was drinking and drugs
You blamed me anytime…
You were unhappy
You tried committing suicide
You failed…
Then, my baby died
This much is true…
A part of me…
Will ALWAYS hate you
Although,
You should know…
In the end…
I'm the one did win

Because I met Him…
My forever…
Someone I wouldn't have met…
If we were still together.
So, I "thank you"…
For leading me to…
A love that's true

Treasure

What is treasure?
Is it diamonds?
Is it gold?
Is it a memory?
Is it a story untold?
Is it something you touch?
Is it something you see?
Is it the thrill of solving a mystery?
Is it a crisp autumn night?
Is it an Eagle taking flight?
Is it vengeance?
Is it wrath?
Is it a warm bubble bath?
Is it an idea?
Is it a dream?
Is it strawberry ice cream?
Is it when you dance?
Is it when you sing?
Is it any or everything?

Grandma

I visited you today
I sat outside your door
You never answered...
So, I watched the rain pour
The sky was weeping...
Just for me
Because you went Home...
In 2018
I visited you today
I had to try again...
I couldn't let the rain win
So, I plead and I pounded...
Again and again
I will not let this nightmare win
I need you...
The family does too...
We are falling apart without you!
I can't continue going on...
Moving to the beat of a heartbreak song
We can trade places
I'll go in your stead
If tomorrow you awaken...
Healthy in bed

Rufus

Day after day
I sit in this cage
Is this forever...
Or just a phase?
Why did they leave?
Come back...please!
I plea...please...
I don't have flees,
I'm a good boy,
And I'll share my toys.
Why did they leave?
Wasn't I enough?
I didn't mean to play rough.
Why did they leave?
Why am I alone?
You were my...forever home.
Why did they leave?
Can you explain?
All they left was heartache and...
An old man's name.
Why did they leave?
One day I asked.
Was told...
"Look toward the future not the past."
So, why did they leave?

Well…now I know.
They left so…
I could become a Romero.

Love is…

I believe in love
I believe love is more than physical
I believe love is emotionally unconditional
I believe love lives past death
I believe you can love with every breath…you
take
I believe love overlooks mistakes
I believe love lights the spark…that is "hope" in
the dark
I believe love comes without shame
I believe love doesn't pass blame
I believe love is a feeling of deep affection
I believe real love takes introspection
I believe you can't love another without loving
yourself
I believe love conquers in sickness and in health.
I believe love is more than lust.
I believe love takes patience and trust.
I believe love is when two become one.
I believe love is for everyone.

Mommy

When you die a piece of me will die too.
It's hard to imagine life without you.
Sometimes you're a mom
Sometimes you're a friend
Always you're someone on whom I can depend
You taught me to advocate for myself
You taught me to fight
You taught me not to fear...what goes...
Bump in the night.
You encouraged my dreams
You supported my passions
You showed me skin care and fashion You
showed me unconditional love
You taught me to pray.
You never gave up when skies were gray
You fought your father in court
Because you loved me more than government
support
When you take that last breath…
When you walk that last mile…
Know when I think of you…I'll smile
You may have passed…
You may be missed…
But I have a lifetime of memories to reminisce

Devil at the Door

Everybody wants to win.
No time to think of what could be lost.
Winning is thrilling
But at what cost?
So much competition
So many ignoring their intuition
So many spreading hate
So many want to segregate…
Separate…
So many don't appreciate…
Those who came before
Those who fought in wars…
Are now living outdoors
Blacks and whites
Are constantly in a fight.
How do you sleep at night?
Is it your loved ones or your pillow you hold
tight?
Do you hold true
The things you claim to value?
Or is it show…
Put on for people you don't know?
So much hurt is spread
So much love is needed
So many pure hearts are impeded

So many search but don't know what they're looking for
Because they're distracted by the devil at the door.

Frienemies

What did I learn from you?
I learned those I trust...can be untrue.
What did I learn from You?
I learned you were someone...I NEVER knew.
What did I learn from you?
I learned who NOT to call when...I'm feeling
blue.
What did I learn from you?
I learned it doesn't matter...what I do.
What did I learn from you?
I learned you were someone I shouldn't
have...given my time to.
What did I learn from you?
I learned I CAN survive on my own two...feet.
What did I learn from you?
I learned to NEVER regret who I meet.
I learned you can't determine how they'll
treat...me
I learned I can't control...someone else's role...
In my life.
I learned to watch for the knife...in my back
I learned friends turn to enemies...like that!

Thanks For Reading

Now I lay me
Down to sleep
I pray this book…
you'll ALWAYS keep
I hope you laughed
Or cried "boo-hoo"
I hope my words…
Touched you
If you hate it…
It's totally fine
It doesn't hurt me…
Because it's your wasted time.

www.ingramcontent.com/pod-product-compliance
Lightning Source LLC
La Vergne TN
LVHW010950200726